D0722218

Make Your Own Art

Drawing

Sally Henry

PowerKiDS press.

New York

Published in 2009 by The Rosen Publishing Group, Inc.
29 East 21st Street, New York, NY 10010

Editor: Alex Woolf
Designers: Sally Henry and Trevor Cook
Consultant: Daisy Fearns
U.S. Editor: Kara Murray

Picture credits: Sally Henry and Trevor Cook

Library of Congress Cataloging-in-Publication Data

Henry, Sally.
  Drawing / Sally Henry.
     p. cm. — (Make your own art)
  Includes index.
  ISBN 978-1-4358-2510-9 (library binding)
  ISBN 978-1-4358-2643-4 (pbk)
  ISBN 978-1-4358-2655-7 (6-pack)
  1. Drawing—Technique—Juvenile literature. I. Title.
  NC655.H46 2009
  741.2—dc22
                           2008011131

Manufactured in China

Contents

Introduction

All artists need to be able to draw. A drawing can work as a finished piece of artwork. It can also be the first step we take when we produce a painting.

Materials

Number 2 and softer **pencils** are useful. Keep a clean **eraser** handy. A good **sharpener** is necessary. Use a scrap of fine **sandpaper** for when you need your pencil really sharp.

Papers with a textured surface are good for tone work. Smooth surfaces are best for line work. Try different textures and colors. Use a stiff-backed **pad** of drawing paper or a **drawing board** for support.

Charcoal can be messy, handle it with care. Use it with a soft or **putty eraser.** Soft pencil and charcoal drawings should be sprayed with **fixative** – a kind of sprayed varnish that will stick everything down to the paper. Always ask an adult to help you when you are using fixative.

Markers with waterproof or water-soluble inks will give quite different results. **Colored pencils** work best on paper with a textured surface. **Wax crayons** are great to use with watercolor paint.

Drawing

A drawing is made of marks. See how many different kinds of straight lines you can make.

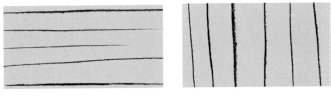

Try horizontal lines. Then draw vertical ones.

Your pencil can make jagged lines with crisp angles. Draw smooth curves. Try tight curves and broad sweeping curves.

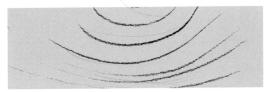

When you draw shapes, try to make your lines describe what you are drawing.

What things do you think these lines belong to?

The car is made of hard metal, so we've given it a hard outline. The sheep has a mostly woolly outline.

Shading

Some shapes need something more to show what they are.

Shading makes this round shape more like a ball. It can cast a shadow, too.

Take time to see what kinds of tone you can get from your pencil. Try soft pencils if you can get them. You can get flatter tones from soft pencils if they are sharpened evenly and you use the side of the lead.

You can use texture to show what something is made of. Layers of texture can also work as shading. We can make things look more solid just by adding the pattern on the surface.

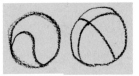

See what your pencil can do. You can make your marks hard to see from a little way away, or you can make them strong enough to be seen from across the room. It's up to you!

Depth

There are lots of different ways to create depth in a picture. We have to use a mix of what we see and what we know. **Overlapping** shows which things are at the front and which are behind.

The eye can see size as distance. A line for the **horizon** will help. Inside, in our picture, the horizon is an imaginary line at eye level. It separates what we look down at and what we look up at.

6 Perspective

We can use **perspective** to draw space, inside and outside. A road or railroad track running directly away from us shows the **vanishing point** on the horizon.

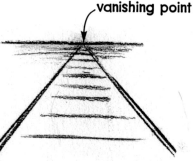

vanishing point

horizon

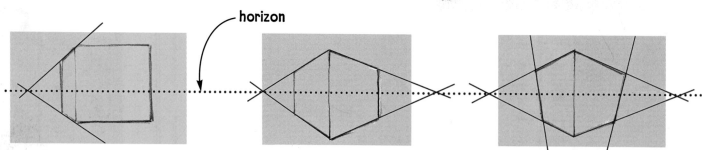

This cube is an example of **one-point perspective**. The lines in the picture converge at the vanishing point.

This **two-point perspective**, shows the cube at an angle to the viewer. There are two vanishing points.

Three-point perspective is more realistic but harder to set up. The horizon and construction lines converge a long way outside the frame.

Frame your view

Cut a rectangular hole about 7 x 5 inches (18 x 13 cm) in a piece of cardboard. Hold it up to find the most interesting view. A similar-sized piece of clear plastic with a grid drawn on it is a good way of separating a view into smaller sections to copy onto similarly squared-up paper.

Proportion and measuring

Whether you draw a view, full-length figures or someone's face, you need to get the proportions right. Judging the relative sizes of things is something that comes with practice, but there are lots of tricks you can use.

- Find some anchor points in your subject. In a big landscape they could be large buildings. In a drawing of a face, they could be the main features, such as the eyes, the nose and the mouth.
- Hold a pencil up at arm's length to measure or compare distances. Use your thumb to fix a distance against the pencil, then move it to another part of the subject to find a matching length.

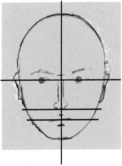

Take care of your work

Always take care of your work. Finishing drawing and cleaning up must include making your work safe for next time or preserving finished work. Charcoal and soft-pencil drawings should be fixed as soon as they are finished. When you sort through drawings, always lift them off each other. Dragging drawings over each other can ruin them.

Keep your finished work in a **folder** – you can easily make this from two sheets of cardboard and some strong tape.

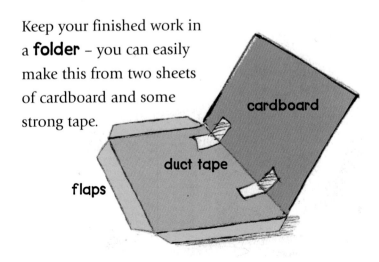

cardboard

duct tape

flaps

Portraits

8

Drawing faces is an excellent way to start. Ask a friend to sit still for you, and tell him or her how long it will take. Try short poses as well as long ones. Change your style based on the time you have. The drawing on the left took half an hour. The one on the right took one minute.

You will need:

- *Tinted or white drawing paper*
- *Soft pencils*
- *Colored pencils or pastels*
- *Markers, white chalk*
- *Soft eraser*

30 MINUTES

What to do...

Drawing 1 is done in brown pencil with white chalk on tinted paper with a textured surface. Drawing 2 is done with a marker on smooth white paper. If you can't get anyone to be a model for you, use a mirror to draw yourself.

2 MINUTES

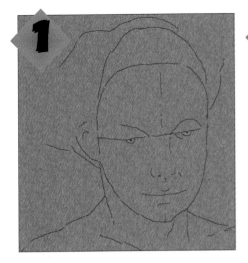

Fix your paper to your board. Build up the head, the hair, the neck and the shoulders in soft brown pencil.

Use a brown pencil to draw the hair, the eyes, the eyebrows and the nose. Put in some shading for the cheeks, the mouth and the chin.

Use white chalk for the highlights and to lighten the background.

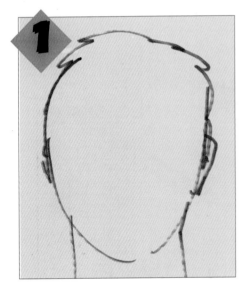

Look very carefully and judge the shape of the head. Try to draw the shape in one try.

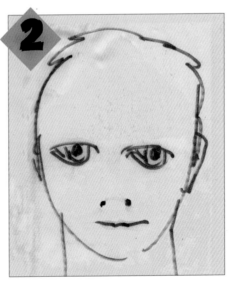

Mark in the centers of the eyes, then draw the eyes and the eyelids. Put dots for the nostrils and just a single line for the mouth.

Sketch in the hairline and the eyebrows. Draw in the shape of the nose, then add lines to complete the mouth.

My Friend

As your drawing skills get better, more friends might agree to be models for you. Ask someone to sit for ten minutes. It will seem like a long time to them, but you will have to work fast!

10 MINUTES   **2 MINUTES**

You will need:

- *Drawing paper*
- *Soft pencil, fine marker*
- *Colored pencils or wax crayons, eraser*
- *A friend to draw*
- *2 chairs*
- *A clock*

What to do...

Get your paper, drawing board and pencils together before your friend arrives. Provide a comfortable chair in a good light. When the model is sitting down, explain that he or she must keep as still as possible for ten minutes. It is useful to have a clock in the room, so you can both see the time. We got our model to listen to music to relax. It worked!

Study the model carefully. Measure the proportions as we suggest on page 7. Use a soft pencil to sketch in some simple outline shapes.

Work quickly and lightly to draw in the features and the hairstyle. Erase any lines you don't need. Keep looking at the model.

Use a fine marker to continue your drawing. We've added more details to the hair, the headphones and the jewelry.

Add shading for the skin color with a colored pencil or wax crayon.

We used a dark crayon to put a texture on the chair to stand out from the clothes.

Hints and Tips

- Sign and date your drawings and record the name of your model.
- Experiment with different pencils, markers and crayons.
- Store your work flat in a folder or large drawer.
- Keep a sketchbook.

Young Animal

Horses are many people's favorite animals. This one is a foal and is not too hard to draw.

You will need:

- Drawing paper
- Pencils, markers
- Eraser
- Coloring supplies

20 MINUTES

What to do...

Set up your drawing board and study step 1. Copy the shapes onto your paper in soft pencil.

5 MINUTES

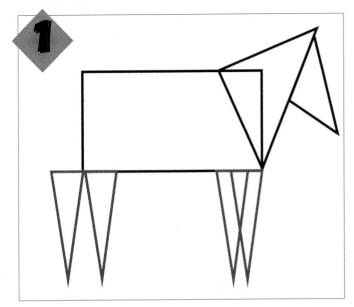

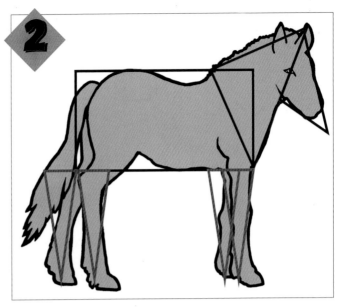

Start with the blue rectangle, then draw four triangles for legs. A green triangle shows his neck and the red triangle shows the head.

Now draw the outline of the horse in pencil over your collection of shapes. When you have got it right, go over the outline with a big marker. Erase the pencil shapes.

Add fine marker lines to show his mane, ears, nose, nostrils and mouth. Draw in the hooves and fetlocks, the hair above the hooves. Color in all areas.

This close-up shows how to color in his eye and add the highlight. Use coloring pens, pencils or crayons to complete your picture.

Still-Life Study

25 MINUTES

5 MINUTES

Drawing a fashionable piece of clothing can often produce interesting results. Here's a much-loved sneaker. We've used soft pencil and blue colored pencil with some colored crayons and a marker.

You will need:

- *Something to draw*
- *Drawing paper*
- *Pencils*
- *Eraser*
- *Colored pencils or crayons*
- *Thick marker*

What to do...

Take your time to get the proportions right at the beginning. If your object has natural parts or surface patterns, like our sneaker, include these in your early drawing. They help to establish its form.

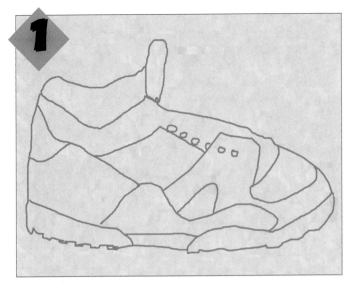

Make your drawing large. There's plenty of detail to fill a bigger piece of paper.

We decided to work with several different blues. The shading picks up the uneven surface of the paper and adds interest to the drawing.

Try out some of the different effects you can get with your colors.

15

Change the angle of your shading to give texture. To complete the drawing, use your darkest blue on the sole areas and the seams. Observation studies like this will help to train your eye.

Look out for rough-textured or tinted paper for your drawings.

Charcoal Sketch

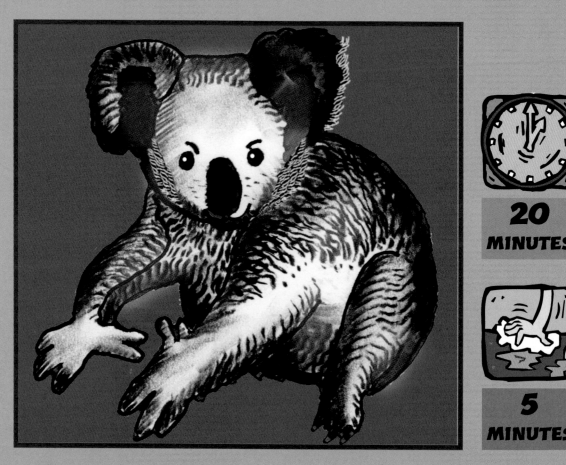

20 MINUTES

5 MINUTES

Nature has many patterns and unusual animals to inspire you!

You will need:

- *Colored paper, fine black marker*
- *Colored chalks or pastels, charcoal*
- *Pencil, putty eraser, fixative*

What to do...

Find something from nature to draw. It could be a feather, a shell, a fossil or a stone. It should have an interesting surface. You could use a photo.

We sketched in some simple shapes to begin.

Draw a bold outline with charcoal to get the shape of his head, body and legs.

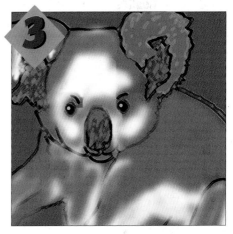

Use charcoal and white chalk to create light and shade. Soften the shading with your fingers.

Add the fur texture with charcoal. Make it denser in the shadows.

Change your marks to show the different kinds of fur.

17

Our fossil is built around a spiral shape. We draw this first.

We draw patterns from the fossil in pale pastel and pencil.

We add some new colors for the different areas of the surface pattern.

You can follow natural colors or use your own imagination to create an image.

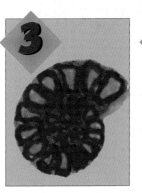

We use greens, pink, ochre, cream and a fine black marker to finish our work.

Cartoons

Our hippo is visiting a water hole with her calf. Baby hippos are just smaller than adults, but without the huge teeth! All hippos love mud and they are great swimmers. There are all sorts of plants near the water. The hippos feed on these at night.

You will need:

- Paper, soft pencil
- Tracing paper
- Thick black marker pen
- Colored markers or paints and a brush

20 MINUTES

What to do...

Cartoon characters need some basic features. Our hippo has her round shape and stumpy teeth!

5 MINUTES

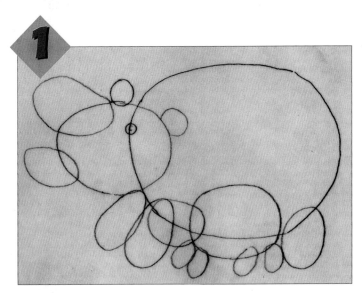

Draw large rounded shapes in soft pencil.

Use the rounded shapes to create the body outline.

Use a thick black marker. This creates a strong drawing.

Add some color with paint or markers.
Draw a water hole background.

Jointed animal figure

You can use wooden models to draw different animals.

Try drawing a toy animal in different positions.

Jungle Wildlife

Even if you have never seen a real jungle, you probably like wildlife. You can let your imagination fly as you think about what you are going to draw now!

You will need:

- *Card stock or paper*
- *Colored markers, soft pencil*
- *Colored pencils or crayons*
- *Nature books, magazines*

40 MINUTES

What to do...

Look in some nature books or magazines to check what certain animals look like. Or you could use your own inspiration. In this fun activity you can create your own jungle for your own animals!

10 MINUTES

1 We have invented a jungle background and drawn a few unusual animals that live there. You can make your own jungle and choose the animals you want to draw.

We started by drawing in soft pencil. Put in some plants and outlines of the bushes. We added grass areas, jungle paths, a stream and a pool.

2 We found it was a good idea to draw and color in our animals first. Then we drew over our pencil jungle outlines with colored markers. This was to show where we wanted to put certain colors.

We filled in the lighter colors first, adding the dark areas of background last. This helps to bring all the bits together.

Here are a few more animals you might find in the jungle.

Stunt Plane

We've chosen to draw a Pitts Special. It's a plane made to do stunts. You can use our drawing, or better still, find a model plane to work from.

You will need:

- Drawing and tracing paper
- Drawing board
- Soft pencil, eraser
- Colored pencils
- Paints, brushes
- Fine waterproof black marker

35 MINUTES

What to do...

This time you can use our picture as a guide. Use tracing paper if you need to mark reference points on the drawing.

5 MINUTES

Draw a guideline (drawn here in red) with a soft pencil. The first line shows the center line of the plane. The body of the plane is called the fuselage. Draw the fuselage as shown.

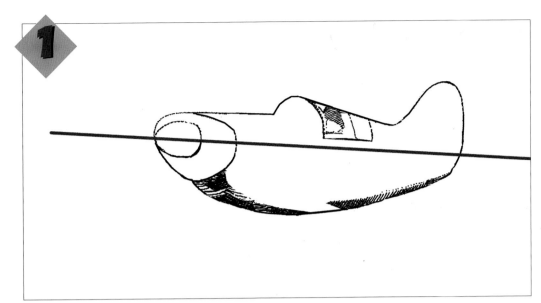

Add three more guidelines. Carefully draw the outlines of the wings and tail. Add the shading on the fuselage. Put in the details of the cockpit and the rudder.

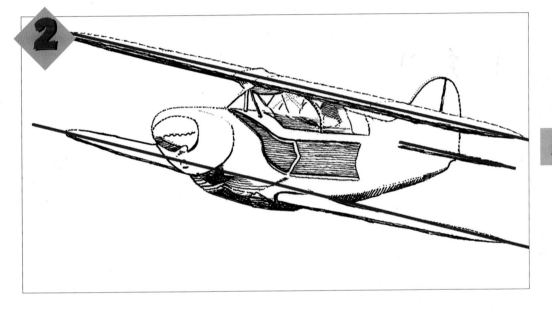

Draw in the main struts, the bottom of the plane, and the exhaust pipe. Erase the guidelines and use a waterproof, fine black marker to draw over your work. You can color your plane like ours or any way you like.

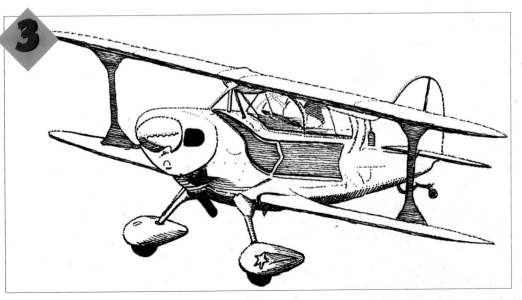

Fantasy Figure

15 MINUTES

5 MINUTES

Now it's time to use your imagination. Think of a fantastic character you'd like to draw.

You will need:

- *Drawing paper*
- *Soft pencil, eraser*
- *Markers, colored pencils*
- *Paintbrushes, paints or colored inks*

What to do...

Follow the steps 1–6 to draw our fantasy wizard and his cat. He would look wonderful on a big poster. Try to find a really large sheet of paper for this drawing.

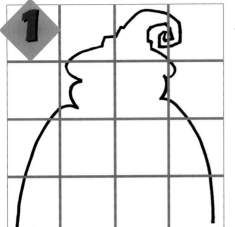

Draw a grid of sixteen squares on a photocopy of the picture opposite. Make a similar grid on your paper. Start your drawing using a pencil. When you get to step 5, you can use a black marker to put bold black lines over your pencil.

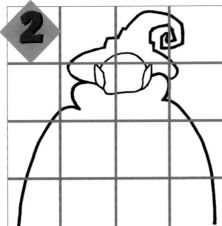

Add his face shape and his ears. See how his collar can be seen once his head is clearer. Now look carefully at the big picture opposite to help with the details.

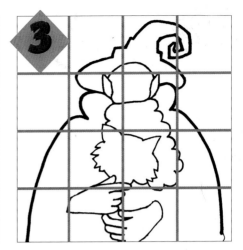

Join his beard onto his face. Copy the position of his hands, using the grid to guide you. Draw in the outline of the cat between his beard and his hands.

Draw in the wizard's eyes and nose. Notice how they are joined together! Put in lines for the sides of the cat's body.

Look again at the large drawing. Put in the eyebrows, the curls, the cat's face, the whiskers, the bracelets, the rings and the details on the wizard's hat.

Add the stars and moons, then use flat color to fill in the line drawing. Use markers, colored pencils, paints or inks. Make the wizard really colorful and fantastical!

Race Cars

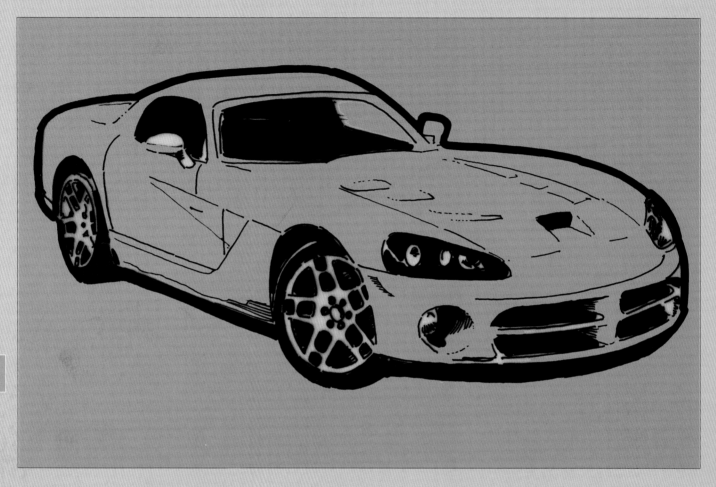

Most people like the look of stylish fast cars. They may seem hard to draw, but if you draw a grid on a photograph or make a careful tracing, you can get great results.

You will need:

- *Photograph of a car*
- *Soft pencil, eraser*
- *Smooth paper*
- *Large-tip black marker*
- *Fine-point black marker*

15
MINUTES

What to do...

Look through some car magazines. You need a picture that shows the whole car. We've cut ours out from its background to make it clearer.

5
MINUTES

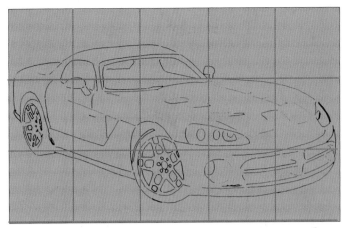

Draw a grid of squares on your photo. Draw a matching grid of faint pencil lines on your paper.

Or you can trace the outline. Using a light touch with your pencil, draw the basic shape.

Use a marker to put in the dark areas in black. Use a fine black marker to add the details.

Use white chalk to show the shiny parts. Put a thick outline around the outside of the whole car.

Try working the other way around, with another car. Use colored paper. Draw a thick outline around the car first. Use a grid to help you.

Use your fine black marker for the details. Put some lines on the windshield in white chalk. Shade in the tires.

Manga Faces

Drawing in the manga style takes years of practice, but here are a few helpful ideas. We've chosen a boy and a girl. We've also shown here five steps for drawing a manga eye. Follow this method when you ink in your work with markers.

You will need:

- *Your favorite manga stories*
- *Soft pencil, eraser*
- *Markers, colored pencils*
- *Paintbrushes and paints*

25 MINUTES

What to do...

Look through your manga books. Study the difference between artists' styles. They all have their own way of showing their subjects' characters.

5 MINUTES

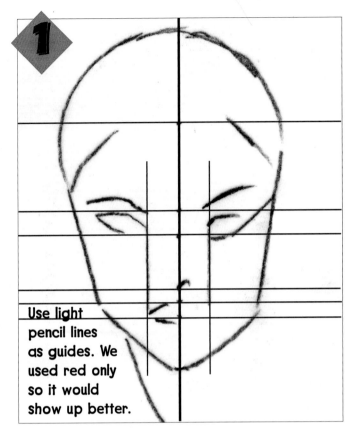

1

Use a pencil to make an oval for her head. Put lines to show where the eyes and mouth go.

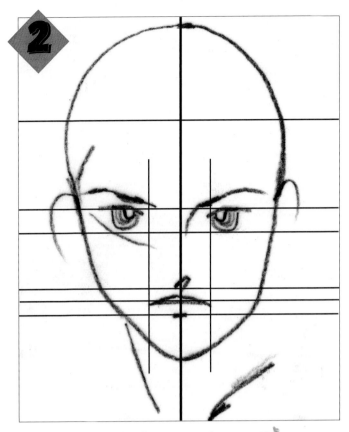

2

Start to put in the basic eye shapes. The eyes are the most important feature of a manga face.

3

This girl has very short hair. Figure out the style.

4

Add more pencil detail before using markers.

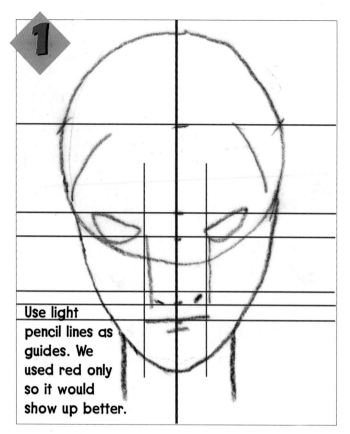

Use a pencil to make an oval for his head. Put lines to show where the eyes and mouth go.

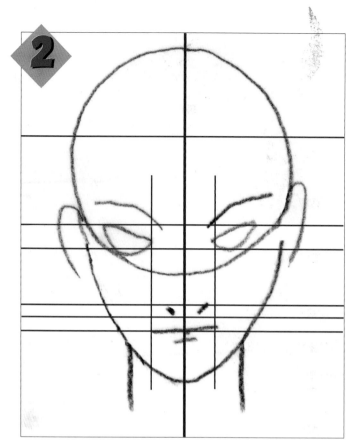

Put in the basic features. The eyes are a key feature of a manga face.

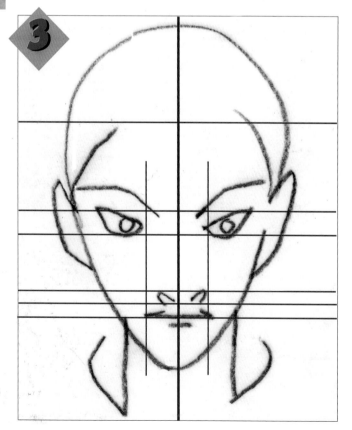

This boy has very pointy long hair and is elfish.

Add more details in pencil. Finish with markers.

jointed figure

Glossary

drawing board   (DRAW-ing BAWRD) A flat piece of plywood or something similar for supporting drawing paper.

fixative   (FIK-suh-tiv) A clear liquid available as a spray for "fixing" work done in pencil, charcoal, chalk or pastels to keep it from smudging.

horizontal   (hor-ih-ZON-til) Going from side to side.

jagged   (JAG-ed) Sharp and uneven.

jointed figure   (JOYNT-ed FIH-gyer) A wooden model with moveable joints used by artists for drawing reference.

layers   (LAY-erz) Thicknesses of things.

materials   (muh-TEER-ee-ulz) What something is made of.

outline   (OWT-lyn) A line drawn around the edges of something.

rectangular   (rek-TAN-gyoo-lur) A shape like a square but longer one way than the other.

seams   (SEEMZ) The lines formed by sewing together two pieces of cloth.

textured   (TEKS-churd) Having a surface that is not smooth.

tracing paper   (TRAYS-ing PAY-per) Thin but strong paper you can see through. Put it on top of something you want to copy and draw on it.

varnish   (VAHR-nish) A liquid, usually clear, for brushing onto finished oil paintings. Paper varnish is also available for drawings.

vertical   (VER-tih-kul) In an up-and-down direction.

31

manga figure

Index

Web Sites

Due to the changing nature of Internet links, PowerKids Press has developed an online list of Web sites related to the subject of this book. This site is updated regularly. Please use this link to access the list:

www.powerkidslinks.com/myoa/draw/